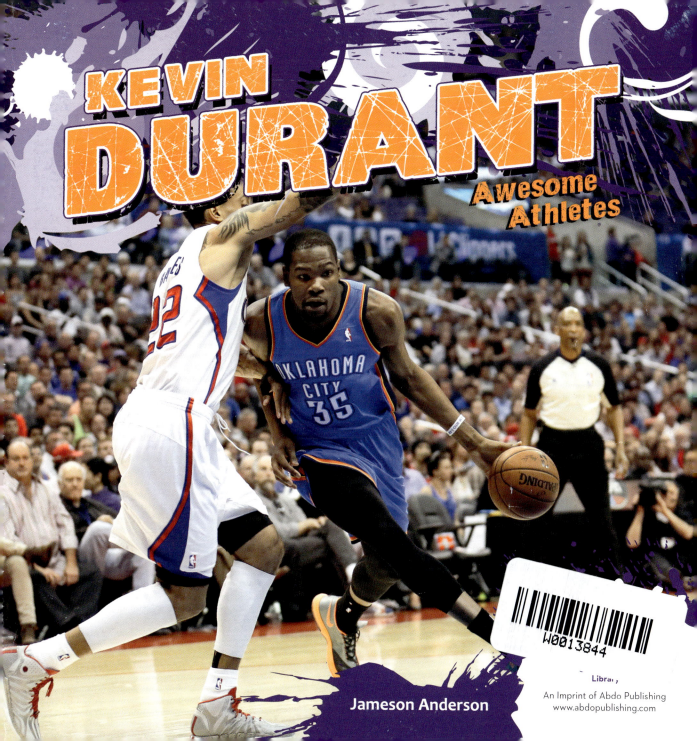

KEVIN DURANT

Awesome Athletes

Jameson Anderson

Library
An Imprint of Abdo Publishing
www.abdopublishing.com

www.abdopublishing.com

Published by Abdo Publishing, a division of ABDO, PO Box 398166, Minneapolis, Minnesota 55439. Copyright © 2015 by Abdo Consulting Group, Inc. International copyrights reserved in all countries. No part of this book may be reproduced in any form without written permission from the publisher. Checkerboard Library™ is a trademark and logo of Abdo Publishing.

Printed in the United States of America, North Mankato, Minnesota.
052014
092014

THIS BOOK CONTAINS
RECYCLED MATERIALS

Cover Photo: AP Images
Interior Photos: AP Images pp. 1, 5, 7, 9, 11, 13, 15, 17, 19, 21, 23, 25, 27, 29

Series Coordinator: Tamara L. Britton
Editors: Rochelle Baltzer
Art Direction: Neil Klinepier

Library of Congress Cataloging-in-Publication Data

Anderson, Jameson.
  Kevin Durant / Jameson Anderson.
     pages cm.
  Includes index.
  ISBN 978-1-62403-329-2
1. Durant, Kevin, 1988---Juvenile literature. 2. Basketball players--United States--Biography--Juvenile literature. 3. African American basketball players--Biography--Juvenile literature. I. Title.
  GV884.D868A63 2015
  796.323092--dc23
  [B]
                      2013048631

TABLE OF CONTENTS

A SPECIAL HONOR

On the night of February 25, 2009, Kevin Durant stood in the Frank Erwin Center at the University of Texas at Austin (UT). It had been two years since Durant played basketball for the Longhorns. On this night, the university was retiring his jersey. No basketball player at UT would again wear the number 35.

Durant left a big mark on the Longhorns' program. Fans would long remember Durant's season when he had 20 double-doubles and scored 30 points in 11 games. He was the first freshman to win the **John R. Wooden Award** and the **Adolph Rupp Trophy**. He was also the first freshman to be named **Naismith College Player of the Year**.

After just one year, Durant left UT for the **National Basketball Association (NBA)**. Experts expected him to continue his outstanding play at the next level. They predicted it wouldn't be long before Durant won the NBA Championship.

Durant and his grandmother Barbara Davis hold his retired jersey. He was just the third player in UT's history to have his jersey retired.

HIGHLIGHT REEL

Kevin Durant was born in Suitland, Maryland.

1988

Durant was named National College Player of the Year; the Seattle SuperSonics made him the second pick in the NBA Draft.

2007

The Thunder met the Miami Heat in the NBA Finals but lost 4–1; Durant won the FIBA championship and an Olympic gold medal.

2012

2006

Durant entered the University of Texas at Austin (UT).

2008

The Sonics moved to Oklahoma City, Oklahoma, and became the Thunder; Durant was named NBA Rookie of the Year.

2014

Durant was named the NBA MVP.

KEVIN DURANT

DOB: September 29, 1988
Ht: 6'9"
Wt: 240
Position: Forward
Number: 35

CAREER AVERAGES:

Assists Per Game: 3.5
Rebounds Per Game: 6.9
Points Per Game: 27.4

AWARDS:

All-Star Game: 2010–2014
All-Star Game MVP: 2012
NBA MVP: 2014
NBA Scoring Champion: 2010, 2011, 2012, 2014
Rookie of the Year: 2008

YOUNG CHAMPION

Kevin Wayne Durant was born on September 29, 1988, in Suitland, Maryland. His parents are Wayne and Wanda Pratt. Kevin has a sister, Brianna, and two brothers, Anthony and Rayvonne. Kevin's father left the family when Kevin was about a year old. Kevin and his siblings lived with his mother and his grandmother Barbara Davis.

Kevin excelled at basketball at a young age. He played with the **Amateur Athletic Union (AAU)** PG Jaguars. He was only 11 years old the first time his team took home a national trophy. Kevin would lead the team to two national championships.

Kevin's AAU coach at the time was Charles Craig. Kevin looked up to Coach Craig and learned a lot from him. Coach Craig died when he was just 35 years old. In memory of his coach, Kevin changed his jersey number to 35. To this day, Kevin's number is 35.

Kevin's grandmother made sure Kevin and his siblings didn't get into trouble when their mother had to work overnight shifts.

SPORTS FOR ALL, FOREVER

THE AMATEUR ATHLETIC UNION (AAU) WAS FOUNDED IN 1888. TODAY, MORE THAN 100,000 VOLUNTEERS WORK WITH 650,000 PARTICIPANTS TO PROMOTE ATHLETIC DEVELOPMENT AND PHYSICAL FITNESS.

EARLY DOUBT

As a student at Drew-Freeman Middle School, Kevin worked hard to improve his game. He practiced at Seat Pleasant Recreation Center. It was ten miles (16 km) away from his house.

In addition, Kevin's coach, Taras Brown, was known for his hard workouts. The grueling practices and long commute were challenging. Sometimes, Kevin slept between practice sessions. He was always tired. He also thought he might be missing out on things other kids were doing.

Kevin loved to play basketball. Yet he wasn't sure that he could put in the work necessary to be a great player. He began to doubt his basketball future. He told Coach Brown he wanted to quit, and he stopped playing.

Kevin's mother helped him through his doubts. Kevin returned to the gym. His game continued to improve. Kevin set a goal to attend a high school with a well-respected basketball program.

Kevin's mother grew up in a tough neighborhood. She wanted more for her children, and she pushed Kevin to work hard for success.

PREP STAR

By the time Kevin was ready for high school, he had good basketball skills. But he wasn't getting the attention of elite high schools. Part of this was because of Kevin's poor grades. He had a weak **academic** record. So, many schools passed on inviting Kevin to play on their teams.

Kevin's **work ethic** had resulted in much success on the court. But he needed to apply it to his schoolwork. So, Kevin enrolled at National Christian Academy in Fort Washington, Maryland.

When he was a junior, Kevin left home for Mouth of Wilson, Virginia. There, he attended Oak Hill Academy. Oak Hill had a nationally recognized basketball program. Kevin gained national exposure when the Warriors' games were shown on ESPN.

But Kevin was far from home. He missed his family. So as a senior, Kevin played at Montrose Christian School in Rockville, Maryland.

FUN FACT NBA STAR FORWARD CARMELO ANTHONY ALSO ATTENDED OAK HILL ACADEMY.

All the years of hard work and practice paid off. Kevin became one of the best high school players in the country. He was named to the 2006 McDonald's All American Team and was the game's co-MVP. In addition, he was named a *USA Today* first team All-American.

The MVP award was given to co-winners Chase Budinger (*left*) and Kevin by legendary basketball coach John Wooden (*center*).

OFF TO TEXAS

Durant finally had the attention of elite basketball schools. The Universities of Connecticut, Kentucky, and North Carolina offered him **scholarships**. But Durant chose UT. There, he was able to start as a freshman.

Not only did he start, but Durant played in every game. The Longhorns finished the 2006–2007 season 25–10. Durant averaged 25.8 points per game and had 20 double-doubles. He also scored more than 20 points in 30 games.

In the Big 12 Tournament, the Longhorns defeated Missouri, Baylor, and Oklahoma State. The team faced Kansas in the final. Though Durant scored 37 points, the Longhorns lost to the Jayhawks 88–84. Durant was named the tournament MVP after scoring a record 92 points.

The Longhorns then headed to the **NCAA** Tournament. On March 16, the Longhorns beat New Mexico State

FUN FACT DURANT WAS THE 2007 BIG 12 PLAYER OF THE YEAR.

79–67. But two days later, they lost to the University of Southern California 87–68 in the second round.

Durant was named the 2007 National College Player of the Year. He knew that he had the skills to play in the **NBA**. A few weeks later, Durant announced he was ready for the NBA **Draft**.

Durant dunks on the Oklahoma State Cowboys in the Big 12 Tournament.

THE NBA

The 2007 **NBA Draft** was held on June 28. The Seattle SuperSonics selected Durant with the second pick in the first round. The Sonics were a struggling team. Discussions with the city of Seattle, Washington, over a new stadium were at a standstill. The team had been sold in 2006. Rumors were it would move to a new city.

The turmoil made it hard to win. The Sonics lost their first eight games. The team finished the 2007–2008 season with a 20–62 record. It was the worst record in team history. Even so, Durant was named NBA **Rookie** of the Year.

Before the 2008–2009 season, the Sonics moved to Oklahoma City, Oklahoma. There, the team would be called the Thunder.

The Thunder started their first season 1–12. Head coach P.J. Carlesimo was fired. The team worked hard to improve. The Thunder finished the season 23–59, a slight improvement from the previous year.

Durant and his family and friends celebrate his Rookie of the Year award.

LEARNING TO WIN

Before the 2009–2010 season, the Thunder acquired better players through trades and the **draft**. The result was immediate. The team won 27 more games than the season before. Durant was named the league's scoring leader. The Thunder finished the season with a 50–32 record and made the **playoffs**.

The team faced the Los Angeles Lakers in the first round. The Thunder lost the first two games in Los Angeles, California. But the team played better in front of their home crowd. They won Games 3 and 4 in Oklahoma City. However, the Lakers matched with two wins back in L.A. and took the series 4–3.

Durant was no longer a good player on a bad team. He was a leader on a winning team. That year, he made his first All-Star Game.

Though guarded closely by Kobe Bryant, Durant scored 32 points in Game 2. But the Lakers squeaked past the Thunder 95–92.

BIG CHANGES

Durant was a big part of the Thunder's success. So, team officials wanted to keep him in Oklahoma City. Before the 2010–2011 season, Durant agreed to a contract that paid him $86 million over five years.

Durant delivered on his end of the deal. The Thunder played to a 55–27 record and made the **playoffs**. In the first game, Durant scored a playoff-high 41 points against the Denver Nuggets. In the final game of the series, Sergi Ibaka blocked nine shots and Durant dropped in 41 points. The Thunder defeated the Nuggets 4–1.

The Thunder faced the Memphis Grizzlies in the next round. The Grizzlies were tough. They had defeated the San Antonio Spurs in the previous round. But the Thunder rolled. The team beat the Grizzlies 4–3, with Durant scoring 39 points in the decisive Game 7.

The Dallas Mavericks awaited the Thunder in the Western Conference Finals. But the Thunder could not duplicate their performance against the Grizzlies. The Mavericks beat the Thunder 4–1.

Durant dunks on Grizzlies forward Zach Randolph for 2 of the 39 points he scored in Game 7.

THE FINALS

The Thunder finished the 2011–2012 season 47–19. The team finished first in its division. Durant led the league in scoring and returned to the All-Star Game. This time, he was named the game's MVP.

In the **playoffs**, the Thunder faced the Dallas Mavericks in the first round. They swept the series in four games.

The Los Angeles Lakers were up next. Durant shined as the Thunder won the first two games. After losing Game 3, the Thunder won the next two and advanced to the Western Conference Finals.

Then, it looked like the Thunder was in trouble. The San Antonio Spurs won the first two games of the next series. But Durant rallied his team back. The Thunder won Games 3 through 6 and a trip to the **NBA** Finals!

Durant watches 2 of his 27 points drop in Game 5 against the Spurs. The series was a rare meeting of the conference's top two seeds.

With victories over the Lakers and Spurs, basketball fans all over the world now knew Kevin Durant. He had become one of the biggest names in the league. However, he would face an even bigger star in the Finals.

In the 2012 **NBA** Finals, Durant and the Thunder faced the Miami Heat and superstar forward LeBron James. The Thunder won the first game of the series behind Durant's 36 points. Hopes were high in Oklahoma City. Fans thought the Thunder might be world champions!

However, the Heat's talent and experience were more than the young Thunder could overcome. The Heat came back to win Games 2 through 5 and take the championship 4–1. Thunder fans were disappointed. Though they lost, they knew that their team had made a lot of progress.

In Game 5, Durant outscored James 32 to 26. But James's triple-double helped lead the Heat to a 121–106 victory over the Thunder.

DOUBLE UP!

IN BASKETBALL, A DOUBLE IS A DOUBLE-DIGIT TOTAL OF POINTS, REBOUNDS, ASSISTS, STEALS, OR BLOCKED SHOTS IN A GAME. A DOUBLE-DOUBLE IS A DOUBLE-DIGIT TOTAL IN TWO OF THESE CATEGORIES. A TRIPLE-DOUBLE IS THE SAME, BUT IN THREE CATEGORIES.

OTHER OPPORTUNITIES

Durant had missed an **NBA** Championship. But that same year he was named to the US National Team. The team competed in the **International Basketball Federation (FIBA)** World Championship. Team USA won the gold medal. It was the team's first world championship since 1994. Durant was named the tournament's MVP.

Durant played on the USA Olympic team at the 2012 Olympic Games in London, England. He set a new basketball record for most points scored in the Olympics. The US team finished undefeated and won the gold medal!

That same year, Durant started the Kevin Durant Family Foundation. This organization raises money to help children and families. In 2013, the foundation donated

$1 million to victims of a tornado that devastated Moore, Oklahoma.

Back in Oklahoma City, the Thunder finished 2012–2013 on top of their division at 60–22. The team again made the **playoffs**. They beat the Houston Rockets 4–2 in the first round. But in the following round, they lost to the Memphis Grizzlies 4–1.

Durant shoots over Brazil's Marcus Vieira in the FIBA tournament. Durant scored 27 points in a 70–68 US victory.

MVP

During the 2013–2014 season, Durant scored at least 25 points in 41 consecutive games. The Thunder ended the season with a 59–23 record. The team again won the division.

The Thunder got past the Memphis Grizzlies and the Los Angeles Clippers in the **playoffs**. The San Antonio Spurs were waiting in the Western Conference Finals. If the Thunder could defeat the Spurs, they would have another shot at the **NBA** Finals.

The Spurs won the first two games of the series. The Thunder came back and grabbed the next two. But the Spurs won the last two games to take the series 4–2.

Once again, Durant would miss the opportunity to win an NBA Championship. Yet his achievements would not go unrecognized. On May 6, 2014, Durant won the league MVP award.

In his MVP acceptance speech, Durant thanked each of his teammates by name. He also praised his mother for her courage and sacrifice toward his success.

When kids dream of playing NBA basketball, they dream of winning a championship. Durant was no different. Ever since he played **AAU** basketball as a boy, Durant has worked to improve his skills. It's only a matter of time until Kevin Durant wins an **NBA** Championship.

GLOSSARY

academic - relating to subjects taught in school, such as reading, writing, and arithmetic.

Adolph Rupp Trophy - an award given each year to the top player in men's NCAA Division I basketball.

Amateur Athletic Union (AAU) - an organization that provides sports programs for participants of all ages and abilities.

draft - an event during which sports teams choose new players.

International Basketball Federation (FIBA) - an association of national organizations that governs international basketball competition.

John R. Wooden Award - an award given each year to the most outstanding men's and women's college basketball players.

Naismith College Player of the Year - an award given each year to the top men's and women's college basketball players.

National Basketball Association (NBA) - a professional basketball league in the United States and Canada. It consists of an Eastern and a Western conference, each with three divisions. There are 30 teams in the NBA.

NCAA - National Collegiate Athletic Association. The NCAA supports student athletes on and off the field. It creates the rules for fair and safe play.

playoffs - a series of games that determine which team will win a championship.

rookie - a first-year player in a professional sport.

scholarship - money or aid given to help a student continue his or her studies.

work ethic - a belief in the benefit and importance of work and its ability to strengthen a person's character.

WEBSITES

To learn more about Awesome Athletes, visit **booklinks.abdopublishing.com**. These links are routinely monitored and updated to provide the most current information available.

INDEX